4-95

Soldiers

NE:

X

D0634827

1916

Philip J. Haythornthwaite

Front cover illustrations:
Canadian troops prepare to
advance; see plate 31.

Back cover illustrations:
Top:
British Mark I tank; see plate
44.

Bottom: Algerian and Tunisian
Tirailleurs; see plate 55.

4/R

1. A French soldier in trench equipment, including goggles and mask over the nose and mouth to protect against gas; waders; and a leather jerkin. The *casque Adrian*, the steel helmet named after its designer, was painted 'horizon blue' and bore an embossed metal badge on the front, for infantry and cavalry a bursting grenade with 'RF' on the ball.

◀1

WORLD WAR ONE: 1916

Philip J. Haythornthwaite

ARMS AND
ARMOUR

▲2 ▼3

▼4

2. A halt on the march: a French infantry company with full field equipment. The 'horizon blue' greatcoat was produced initially double-breasted for infantry and single-breasted with longer skirts for cavalry; almost immediately a second infantry version appeared, as here, single-breasted and with breast-pockets, here without the usual unit-numbers carried on the collar-patches. Note the spare boots tied to the sides of the knapsack. The smaller haversacks are probably containers for the gas mask.

3. The 'Blue Devils' in a new guise: a picket of French *Chasseurs Alpins* in the Vosges. These élite mountain troops were renowned for their dark blue berets, but although here some retain their dark blue tunics and perhaps white trousers, their head-dress is now the universal *casque Adrian*. Shown clearly on the man at the right is the 1886-pattern Lebel bayonet with white-metal hilt, narrow cruciform blade and downswept quillon, the latter being removed to produce the 1916 pattern.

4. A French trench mortar positioned in a sandbagged emplacement near a dug-out, typical of those in which the defenders of Verdun existed. Three basic types of mortar were employed at this time: the 1915 58mm and the later 240mm and 340mm varieties. The projectile about to be inserted into the barrel has tail-fins to provide stabilization in flight, leading to the nickname 'aerial torpedo'. Note the carpet of branches performing the same function as British duckboards.

INTRODUCTION

First published in Great Britain in 1990 by Arms and Armour Press, Villiers House, 41-47 Strand, London WC2N 5JE.

Distributed in the USA by Sterling Publishing Co. Inc., 387 Park Avenue South, New York, NY 10016-8810.

Distributed in Australia by Capricorn Link (Australia) Pty. Ltd, P.O. Box 665, Lane Cove, New South Wales 2066. Australia.

British Library Cataloguing in Publication Data
Haythornthwaite, Philip J. (Philip John), 1951–
World War One: 1916. – (Fotofax).
1. World War 1
I. Title II. Series
940.3
ISBN 1-85409-002-X

Designed and edited by DAG Publications Ltd. Designed by David Gibbons; edited by Roger Chesneau; layout by Anthony A. Evans; typeset by Typesetters (Birmingham) Ltd. and Ronset Typesetters Ltd.; camerawork by M&E Reproductions, North Fambridge, Essex; printed and bound in Great Britain by The Alden Press, Oxford.

After the horrors of 1915, the abortive expedition to the Dardanelles and the advent of trench warfare and poison gas, the wretchedness multiplied in 1916. The war widened a stage further by the entry of Roumania into the conflict, and operations in the Middle East intensified with the Arab Revolt. Despite a successful Russian drive on the Eastern Front (the cost of which contributed to the upheaval of 1917) and a serious reverse in Mesopotamia, the Allies' main effort in 1916 was concentrated on the Western Front, centered around the French attempts to hold Verdun and the British Somme offensive initiated partly to relieve pressure on the beleaguered French. The attack of 1 July 1916 was the costliest day in the history of the British Army, yet the 60,000 casualties it sustained were only the beginning of an unbelievably sanguinary struggle which dragged on into early winter, causing about one and a quarter *million* casualties and destroying some of the best elements of the armies of both combatants. It also ushered in a new era of military tactics, that of the armoured fighting vehicle. Like the Dardanelles expedition, the development of the tank had been intended to break the deadlock of the war on the Western Front; against a less resolute enemy it might have done, but by the end of the year the terrible stalemate of trench warfare was once again in place.

In the development of military costume and equipment, 1916 witnessed fewer changes than the previous years apart from the advent of the tank, though by the end of the year steel helmets, virtually unknown at the outbreak of war, were almost universal, with the French Adrian pattern spreading to many of the Allied nations, the German 'coal-scuttle' being used by the Central Powers and the British 'tin hat' by the troops of the Empire. Light machine-guns came into greater prominence, providing immediate fire-support for each company, and with patterns such as the Lewis and Chauchat being immeasurably more mobile than the heavy machine-guns, the latter now took on the role almost of light artillery. In addition to the concentration of artillery fire providing bombardments of unimaginable intensity, 'trench artillery' was now more fully developed with the widespread use of the 'Tock-Emma' (T/M: trench mortar).

Of the many thousands of photographs published at the time in contemporary books and periodicals such as the *Illustrated War News*, *Sphere* and similar illustrated magazines, a greater degree of censorship and propaganda may be encountered in the publications of all nations, and thus contemporary captions should be regarded with a degree of circumspection. Throughout this series it is intended that the central data section should provide a chronology of the year in question, and concentrate upon the arms and equipment of one of the main combatant nations, in this case the German Army.

5. A French trench near Maurepas, the defenders of which wear the 'horizon blue' tunic in place of the greatcoat. Like most armies, the French used a number of patterns of hand-grenade, including spherical, racket (on a wooden handle like a table-tennis bat), egg-grenades with smooth casing such as the Modèle 1915, cylindrical incendiaries like the Modèle 1916, and these fragmentation grenades with short handle and segmented casing to explode into shrapnel. The narrow tin box worn on a shoulder-strap by the man in the foreground is the container for the 'Tissot' gas mask.

6. French infantry drawing drinking-water for their company from a 'dump' a short distance behind the lines. The availability of fresh water was often limited in the front line, and supplies often had to be carried manually from such central points. The water was sometimes carried in barrels on the shoulder, or in this case in tins; one man wears a rain-cape and the other a sleeveless jerkin over his greatcoat.

▲5 ▼6 ▲7

7. French cooks and cook-wagon at Verdun. All wear the 'horizon blue' tunic in preference to the greatcoat (which at the start of the war was the almost universal upper garment) and the steel *casque Adrian*, one with a knitted balaklava helmet underneath. The filthy state of these men is typical for the campaign (even though they were responsible for preparing food), and the unshaven appearance makes the nickname *poilu* ('hairy one') more than usually appropriate!

8. Close-quarter trench fighting produced a number of bizarre and anachronistic uniforms, such as the improvised breastplate worn by this French infantryman at Verdun; others used steel bucklers (shields) in the hope of deflecting German bullets. Note the gong made from a shell-case hanging from the trench wall; when struck it acted as a warning of poison gas.

9. Under bombardment trench-systems could disappear into a series of half-filled gullies and hollows, as here: French troops shelter from the artillery fire which is doubtless the cause of the debris visible. Like that in the background, some shells exploded with a cloud of black smoke, hence the British nickname 'coal-box' for such projectiles.

10. The staff uniform of the French Army is illustrated in this portrait of 'Butcher' Mangin, who planned and directed the recapture of Forts Douaumont and Vaux at Verdun. Charles Marie Emmanuel Mangin (1866–1925) was one of the most capable, and certainly most fearless, of France's generals; trained in colonial warfare, he had the highest regard for the French African troops. Although he was prepared to sacrifice any number of men to attain his objectives, he was as careless of his own safety as that of his troops. He wears the 'horizon blue' tunic and breeches with black breeches-stripe, gilt stars above the cuff (indicative of general officers' rank, two to seven according to grade), the dress kepi with dark-blue band, scarlet top and gold embroidery, and brown leather belt and boots.

11. Verdun was supplied by a 40-mile minor road known as the *Voie Sacrée* (sacred way), supplies being brought up by convoys of lorries; but mule-trains were still used, like that halted here for refreshments. These mules carry machine-gun ammunition in 'racks'; French guns such as the Model 1905 'Puteaux' and Model 1907 'St-Etienne' used rigid metal bands holding 25 cartridges. Only one of the men illustrated wears the steel helmet; except when under fire, the kepi was often preferred for its greater comfort.

12. Crown Prince Wilhelm of Germany behind the wheel of his staff-car on the Verdun Front, where he was in nominal command. 'Little Willie's' uniform illustrates a practice, adopted by numerous German generals, of wearing regimental rather than staff uniform: though the motoring goggles conceal the lower black-and-white Prussian cockade on the cap, the upper badges identify the uniform as that of the 1st *Leib*-Hussars (of which he was colonel): a black cap with scarlet band, silver piping, and the national red/white/black cockade over a silver skull and crossed bones, the regimental badge.

▲10　▼11

13. Until the issue of the steel helmet in mid-1916, the German Army continued to wear the *Pickelhaube* with field-grey cloth cover. This searchlight section (the light hung around the neck of one of the crew) wears the 1910-pattern field-grey tunic with 'Swedish' cuffs as used by the Guards, field artillery, most supporting services and a minority of infantry regiments. The *Unteroffizier* in the centre has rank indicated by the lace around the collar. The pouches on the waist-belts are the 1895-pattern, which continued in use despite the introduction of the 1909 multiple pouches, and jackboots are worn; though puttees were used from this period, they were never universal.

14. The German Army began to receive the steel helmet in the early summer of 1916, of the distinctive 'coal-scuttle' shape, with a frontal reinforcing plate for lookouts. The 1910-pattern field-grey tunic (*Waffenrock*) was amended in 1915 when a turned-back deep cuff was introduced and the piping on the rear skirts removed. A new garment, the *Bluse*, was authorized in September 1915, with simpler decorations and the breast-buttons concealed by a fly-front; but in practice all three patterns were worn simultaneously, so that the earlier tunics could still be encountered at the end of the war. The officer here wears the 1910-pattern tunic with 'Brandenburg'-style flapped cuffs; the others wear the amended version with plain cuffs.

15. A German water-cart at a village well. The purity of water in front-line areas could not always be guaranteed, hence the chalked notice on the cart, *Nur Trinkwasser*. The chimney affixed to the cart led to mobile stoves and cook-carts being nicknamed *Gulasch-Kanone* ('stew-guns'), for when stowed for movement the chimney resembled the barrel of a fieldpiece. The men here wear the 1910-pattern *Waffenrock*; the coloured piping on the rear skirts shows clearly on that of the man operating the well-wheel, and the man to his left has 'Swedish' cuffs with *Garde-Litzen* (lace loops, normally white with a central red line), the insignia of the Foot Guards, grenadiers and certain other infantry units.

16. German infantry wearing the field cap and field-grey greatcoat. The man at the left retains the large collar-patches officially abolished in September 1915. The shoulder-strap identified the regiment (so that Allied raiding-parties were instructed to carry away any straps they encountered to identify the units opposing them); the straps were of the garment-colour with the regimental number usually in red, sometimes with piping (generally white for infantry); in this case it bears the scarlet '102' of the 3rd Saxon Regiment, *Infanterie-Regt. Nr. 102 (König Ludwig III von Bayern)*. The man at the right is from a regiment which bore a badge on its straps, in this case a crown which, with the *Garde-Litzen* loops on the tunic collar, would seem to indicate the 1st Baden Grenadiers (*Badisches Leib-Grenadier Regt. Nr. 109*).

17. The ordinary German service dress: the 1910-pattern tunic, some at least with 'Brandenburg' cuff-patches, and the soft cloth field cap with coloured band and national (upper) and state (lower) cockades; a number of men have the coloured band concealed by a strip of field-grey cloth, common practice in the front line. The man in the immediate foreground wears the peaked field cap which could be worn by all ranks off-duty but was generally restricted to officers and senior NCOs.

▲14 ▼15

16 ▲

17 ▲

18. German infantrymen photographed in France, wearing the field cap and illustrating the simultaneous use of the 1910-pattern *Waffenrock* with 'Brandenburg' cuff-flaps and the 1915 amended pattern with deep, plain cuffs; the 1915 *Bluse* was similar to the latter but with the breast-buttons concealed by a fly-front. The field-grey cap (*Mütze*) had the band and upper piping in the arm-of-service colour (most infantry red, artillery black, *Jägers* light-green, train light-blue, etc.) with circular metal cockades, the national red/white/black at the top and the state cockade on the band, the latter often concealed by a strip of field-grey cloth. The tunic-buttons were produced either in matted metal or were painted field-grey.

18 ▼

Highlander (centre) and Lowlander (right) wear the khaki 'Tam-o'-Shanter' and the ordinary khaki tunic (the Highland 'doublet' pattern was rarely seen by this period), the Highlander with the 1914-pattern leather equipment; note the cover on his rifle, the others having the bolt-mechanism exposed. The flowers worn by all three were sold for charity on 'Alexandra Day' (named after Queen Alexandra), 21 June 1916.

20. A British infantry corporal on sentry duty on the Western Front. Although this shows the uniform and 1908-pattern equipment to good effect, it was probably posed for the photographer some distance from the front line: the rifle has a rag around it to exclude dirt, and at the 'front' the loophole would probably have had a sacking cover so as not to show light through and thus not attract a sniper.

21. War service was not restricted to the young; illustrated here in the uniform of the 8th (Ardwick) Battalion of the Manchester Regiment in 1916 is Corporal C. E. Madeley,

▲19 ▼20

19. Returning to the 'Front': British soldiers at Victoria Station, London, at the end of their leave (when weapons were carried). This illustrates the diversity of British uniform: the private of the Machine-Gun Corps (left) wears ordinary service uniform and 1908-pattern web equipment; the lanyard is a unit addition. The

▼21

an ecclesiastical stained-glass craftsman from Manchester. He was accepted for the 8th Manchesters in 1915 on account of his service with the Manchester Rifle Volunteers, which he joined in 1870, being aged 61 at the time of his enlistment; his son also served in the regiment.

22. The alteration of uniform which occurred during the war is demonstrated by the photograph here of Scottish Highlanders. This depicts the regulation uniform of a 2nd lieutenant, the tunic cut in 'doublet' shape, unique to kilted regiments, with rank-insignia borne upon 'gauntlet' cuffs; with kilt, hose, glengarry cap, drab spats and the sporran, the latter omitted on active service.

23. No greater contrast could be imagined than that of the regulation 'Highland' uniform and that illustrated here: only the head-dress is distinctive, the khaki serge Balmoral or 'Tam-o'-Shanter' bonnet which replaced the glengarry in 1916, here with the badge of the Seaforth Highlanders. The remainder of the uniform is entirely 'English': it is supposed that some units of the 51st (Highland) Division received ordinary trousers and puttees in 1916, in which Division the 4th–6th Battalions Seaforth Highlanders served in that year.

24. On 27 March 1917 the 1st Battalion Northumberland Fusiliers and 4th Battalion Royal Fusiliers (9 Brigade, 3rd Division) captured an enemy salient at St-Eloi. This shows the celebrations of victory, displaying German shakos (the one worn by the man seated at right apparently having a service dress fabric cover but with the plate affixed outside), a German gas mask and field-cap. The captain in the background wears the red cross brassard of medical personnel; the 7th, 8th and 142nd Field Ambulances were attached to the 3rd Division at this date.

22 ▲   23 ▲   24 ▼

25. A private of the London Scottish, wearing the regimental uniform as part of 168 Brigade, 56th Division (red triangle on upper sleeve). The tunic has the rounded skirts of 'doublet' pattern, and bears two wound-stripes on the lower sleeve. The khaki Tam-o'-Shanter was adopted by the unit (14th London Regiment) in spring 1915, with blue backing to the regimental badge and a blue 'tourie' (pompom). The kilt is of the regimental 'Hodden grey' colour, and the hose-tops similar, with blue 'flashes'; on active service puttees were preferred to the spats. The belt is from the 1908 web equipment; but for the removal of the sporran and the addition of a khaki kilt-apron, this is the uniform worn on active service.

26. The London Scottish on the march, wearing a mixture of ordinary tunics and 'doublets' with rounded skirts, khaki aprons and helmet covers. For a time after the issue of the steel helmet in March 1916 the regiment wore blue pompoms on the helmet covers, until it was realized that these were revealing the unit's identity to the enemy. Despite active service conditions, the officer in the foreground retains his sporran, and appears to have web equipment instead of the usual 'Sam Browne' belt; the medical party in the foreground carry a rolled stretcher, their white brassards on the left upper arm bearing the letters 'SB' (stretcher-bearer).

▲25   ▼26

27. No offensive could have been contemplated without an immense preliminary bombardment; the amount of artillery deployed by both sides on the Western Front was astonishing. This British howitzer is 'dug-in', such a pit being usable due to the breech-mechanism which absorbed recoil, without which the gun would have been driven backwards many yards by the discharge of each shell. The poles support camouflage-netting to conceal the position from German aerial observation.

28. Canadian infantry in a trench in which corrugated iron is used as wall-supports and dug-out roof; note also the slatted wooden 'duckboards' to provide firmness underfoot. One of the men uses a trench periscope, of which many varieties existed; the man at the extreme right wears gumboots instead of puttees, the corporal at the left has a raincoat, and the man next to him a sleeveless leather jerkin.

29. Lunch in the trenches: three Canadians in the front line. The uniform is like that of the British Army; note the leather jerkin and small pouch for the gas mask worn by the man at the right, and the 'C/5' regimental collar-insignia of the man at the left. Very prominent is a rum-jar, a common feature in the trenches as rum was issued regularly to combat the cold and dampness. The jars were made of buff earthenware with a dark-brown glazed neck, and bore the letters 'S R D' (Special Ration Department), which with their usual humour the troops said indicated 'Seldom Reaches Destination'!

27 ▲   28 ▼

29 ▼

▲30 ▼31

▲32

30. 'C' Company, 1st Battalion Lancashire Fusiliers fixes bayonets, supposedly immediately before the attack of 1 July 1916. The officer (second right) wears a less conspicuous ordinary tunic with rank badges on the shoulder-strap and the battalion crimson-and-yellow diamond insignia on his back below the collar. Yellow flashes on the left of each helmet represents the regiment's traditional yellow hackle; the shoulder-straps bear a brass grenade over 'LF', and the red triangle of the 29th Division is worn on each upper sleeve. Just visible on the pack of the corporal at the left, below the blade of his entrenching-tool, is a tin triangle, used as a recognition-symbol of rank for the men following. The man at the right has the crown insignia of company sergeant-major on the lower sleeve. This one attack cost the battalion a staggering 486 casualties.

31. 'Fix bayonets!': Canadian troops prepare to advance. Note that they are equipped with the British Lee-Enfield rifle instead of the Canadian Ross, the latter a weapon of great accuracy but so prone to becoming fouled that by 1916 most had been withdrawn, only a limited number being retained for sniping.

32. Roll-call of the 2nd Battalion Seaforth Highlanders at the end of the first day of the Somme attack. Note the khaki kilt-aprons and the large white letter 'C' stitched to the upper sleeve, a battalion-identification sign worn especially for the attack of 1 July. Less clearly visible is the triangle of Mackenzie tartan on the upper sleeve, and the coloured patches on the khaki helmet covers used by the 4th Division to identify the brigade: green, yellow and red respectively for the 10–12 Brigades, and horizontal bar, vertical bar, square and diamond for the 1st–4th battalions of each brigade. As the second battalion of 10 Brigade the 2nd Seaforths wore

a green vertical bar; a green diamond was the sign of the 2nd Royal Dublin Fusiliers (fourth battalion, 10 Brigade), and so on.

33. 'Over the top': British infantry leaving the trenches to support the attack on Morval. Visible in the far distance is a line of troops, illustrating the excellent target they presented to the Germans when attacking in this manner. Note the different methods of carrying equipment; the small pouches slung over the shoulder contain the cotton 'PH' (Phenate-Hexamine) gas helmet.

34. German prisoners under escort near Thiepval. This illustrates the variety of uniform encountered on the Western Front: the British escorts have a mixture of 1908 web equipment and the 'emergency' 1914-pattern leather equipment; the narrow strap over the shoulder supports the cotton pouch for the 'PH' gas helmet. The German with the bandaged head wears the ribbon of the Iron Cross at his neck.

▲37

35. German prisoners at Contalmaison, July 1916. Several of the escorting British troops have additional cartridge-bandoliers slung over the shoulder (cotton bandoliers with 50 extra rounds were issued before the great attack of 1 July). The Germans – some of whom appear not unhappy at being captured – wear the field cap: the steel helmet was heavy and not as popular as the soft cap. All appear to wear the 1910 *Waffenrock* with 1915 modification, and have the white *Garde-Litzen* loops on the collar.

36. German casualties and prisoners await evacuation during the great British attacks of July 1916. Those in the foreground wear the 1910 tunic with 'Brandenburg' (flapped) cuffs, despite the 1915 modification and the introduction of the *Bluse* in that September. The shoulder-strap of the man seated right identifies the unit as the 38th Silesian Fusiliers (*Füsilier-Regt. Graf Moltke, Schlesisches, Nr. 38*). Both German and British medical personnel are shown, the former with a red cross

▲35 ▼36

brassard and the latter with a red cross badge on the upper sleeve. The 'Tommy' in the foreground – resembling Bairnsfather's immortal 'Old Bill' – dispenses refreshment from what appears to be the regulation rum-jar.

37. The artillery bombardments on the Western Front exceeded anything that had occurred in the past: this is the main street of Guillemont, captured from the Germans on 3 September 1916. Much of the Somme battleground was reduced to this level of utter devastation.

38. Canadians returning from the front line in typically mud-plastered condition. The man on the left wears his helmet over a woollen 'cap comforter', and has a jerkin over his tunic; the other has a civilian-style cardigan under his tunic. Both have waterproof legwear, waders or gumboots.

39. A British Rolls-Royce armoured car stops at a dressing-station near Guillemont. Both horse-drawn and motor ambulances (that in the foreground a Daimler) are parked amid the barren, shell-

torn terrain; visible in the extreme background is apparently a stretcher-party bringing in another casualty. Note the padre to the right of the armoured car, wearing officers' service dress plus clerical collar.

38▲   39▼

▲40 ▼41

40. A British 'CCS' (casualty clearing-station) behind the front line, the injured on stretchers awaiting evacuation; rudimentary treatment would have been given at advanced dressing-stations which went by a number of titles including 'RAP' (regimental aid post). The staff here are medical orderlies, doctors and chaplains. This is one of the better stations; many were situated within the range of enemy shelling and in appalling and muddy terrain.

41. Cynics remarked that 'walking wounded' have every reason to look cheerful, for a 'Blighty one' (an injury necessitating evacuation to Britain) removed them from the horrors of the firing-line. This group of injured Canadians includes a Japanese serving with the Canadian army, and a member of the 16th Battalion, Canadian Expeditionary Forces (British Columbia Scottish) whose glengarry bears the regimental badge of a crowned saltire with '16' over a scroll inscribed '*Deas Gu Cath*'. Note the tunics with more than the usual British five buttons down the breast, and the labels giving details of initial treatment, identity, etc.

42. British infantry just returned from duty in the front line; the man at the right has brought back only half his rifle and has his equipment festooned around him (note the mess-tin). He wears his 'tin hat' on top of the service cap, and both men have improvised capes from what appear to be blankets as some protection from the rain which is evident from the muddy ground.

43. A 'wiring party' of British infantry. Stringing barbed wire was a hazardous operation, especially as it was often conducted within range of the enemy and often at night. The corkscrew-like implements carried by the man at the head of the party are stanchions upon which the wire was strung. In the foreground is a large coil of wire and what appears to be a water-pump.

44. Probably nothing changed the nature of war more than the advent of the tank, first deployed on 15 September 1916 at Flers-Courcelette. The British Mark I tank came in two varieties: 'male' with two naval 6pdr guns, and 'female' with Hotchkiss machine-guns mounted in sponsons bolted to each side. Crew comprised a commander, driver, two gearsmen and four gunners.

42 ▲   43 ▲   44 ▼

The large wheels at the rear were intended to facilitate minor changes of course (proper steering was by changing gear on the tracks, which operated independently) and were subsequently discarded. Despite a top speed of less that 4mph and limited range, the initial effect of these 28-ton monsters was devastating; though prone to become bogged down, they could have played a major role had they been deployed in sufficient numbers.

45. Each battalion maintained its transport section, crewing motor vehicles and mule- or horse-drawn wagons. This battalion transport cadre of the East Lancashire Regiment have the ordinary uniform with the addition in some cases of cavalry legwear; the lance-corporal (second right) wears riding-breeches and laced leather gaiters, but others have had to improvise, such as the man at the extreme right with socks pulled up over the trouser-leg.

45 ▼

GERMAN HELMET PLATES AND RANK INSIGNIA

▲a.   ▼b.

▲d.   ▼e.

▼c.

▼f.

Many different variations on the standard head-dress plate existed in the German Army, of which a representative selection is illustrated here, most obviously the 'state' plates of non-Prussian units, but many regimental patterns also existed:

a. The standard Prussian 'line eagle' *Pickelhaube*-plate with

motto *'Mit Gott Fur Koenig und Vaterland'*.
b. The same basic plate with the addition of a *Landwehr* cross insignia, indicative of a reserve or *Landwehr* battalion.
c. The 'Guard eagle' with outstretched wings, without the 'Guard Star' on its breast (the star of the Order of the Black Eagle, which featured on most Guard badges): this

version worn by the 2nd, 3rd and 8th Grenadiers and 1st and 3rd Dragoons.
d. Plate of the 13th and 14th *Uhlans* bearing the battle-honours 'Peninsula', 'Waterloo' and 'Garzia Hernandez' gained by the forebears of these units when part of the British King's

German Legion.
e. The 'dragoon eagle' with upstretched wings, with the 'Waterloo' honour of the 16th (Hanoverian) Dragoons.
f. Busby (*Pelzmütze*) badge of the 7th Hussars, which bore the title 'King Wilhelm's', hence the 'WR I' cipher.

g. The Saxon state plate of the arms of the kingdom in silver on a brass or gilt 'sunburst'.

h. A similar plate with the *Landwehr* cross in silver behind the coat of arms, indicative of a reserve battalion.

i. A typical infantry shoulder-strap, the primary method of identifying the unit, red numerals on field-grey, in this case of the *Niederrheinisches Füsilier-Regt. Nr. 39*, from Düsseldorf.

j. Officers' shoulder-strap pattern, silver and black braid on branch-coloured backing (here scarlet) with gilt badges, the grenade and number indicating a *Leutnant* of the 66th (4th Baden) Field Artillery.

k. Officers' dress rank-insignia: gilt-crescented epaulettes with padded cloth centres in the branch-colour. Left: *Leutnant*, 66th (4th Baden) Field Artillery; right, *Hauptmann* (captain), Medical Corps.

l. Field officers' epaulettes had bullion fringes: with no rank-badge, major, here of *Infanterie-Regt. von Horn (3 Rheinisches) Nr. 29*, from Trier. Other rank-badges were: *Oberleutnant*, one star; field ranks with twisted braid straps or fringed epaulettes, *Oberstleutnant* (lieutenant-colonel) with one star and *Oberst* (colonel) with two.

g.▲

h.▲

i.▲ k.▼

j.▲ l.▼

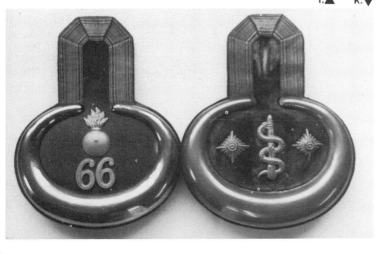

CHRONOLOGY: 1916

1915 had seen the extension of the theatre of war to include the Middle East, and a widening of the campaigning in Europe. The Western Front remained deadlocked, and would be the focus of the major Allied effort in 1916; the Caucasus and Italian Fronts similarly remained without decisive advantage, though on the Eastern Front the Central Powers were in the ascendant, the Serbian Front had virtually collapsed (the Allies clinging to Salonika), and the Allied expeditions to the Dardanelles and in Mesopotamia were in a parlous position. Thus far, the Allies had not enjoyed the success they envisaged when the war commenced almost a year and a half before.

The Dardanelles

8–9 January: After untold privation and immense casualties, the Allied expedition to the Dardanelles was withdrawn without the loss of a man, in sharp contrast to the mismanagement of the landings. The cessation of operations in the Gallipoli theatre enabled the Western Allies to concentrate their efforts on the Western Front.

The Western Front

Both sides determined to make a major effort along the Western Front. France was beginning to experience a serious drain on manpower, so that the Germans hoped that even if they were unable to break the Allied defences, they could reduce France to a situation of desperation. Masterminding the Allied strategy, Joffre attempted to overcome the lack of co-ordination which had bedevilled Allied plans in 1915 by organizing a concerted offensive in the West, East and Italy, intended to take place towards the middle of the year, by which time Russia would be prepared.

February-December: Verdun. The German assault was launched long before that planned by the Allies, directed towards the fortified French position around Verdun. From 21 February massive German attacks drove the French from part of their defences, including Fort Douaumont; Joffre appointed General Henri Philippe Pétain to hold Verdun at all costs. From the outset Pétain's policy was exemplified by his statement *Ils ne passeront pas* (they shall not pass) — a marked difference from the attitude he adopted in 1940 — and when the next German assault occupied more territory (6 March) he counter-attacked and recovered it. This was the pattern for the remainder of the battle, the French clinging on grimly, supplied only by the *Voie Sarée* (sacred way), a 40-mile minor road which was their only route for reinforcement. A third German drive was resisted in April/May, until in June/July the French were reduced almost to the point of defeat, with the loss of Fort Vaux on 9 June; yet they hung on until demands for reinforcement on the Eastern Front caused the Germans to transfer 15 divisions, and by early September the Germans realized that their resources were insufficient to break Verdun and switched to the defence. The French then counter-attacked and recaptured Forts Douaumont (24 October) and Vaux (2 November), so that by the end of the year almost all the captured territory had been regained. The horror of Verdun had accomplished little save the loss of more than 540,000 French and 430,000 German troops.

1 July–November: The Somme. Joffre's planned Anglo-French offensive was amended to a primarily British assault due to the immense pressure upon the French at Verdun. The main attack was launched on 1 July by General Henry Rawlinson's Fourth Army, with Edmund Allenby's Third Army farther north, against heavily-prepared German defences. The initial attack was the blackest day in the history of the British Army, which lost about 60,000 men on 1 July; it was especially terrible in the involvement of new battalions raised within a small locality — for example those units styled 'Pals' — so that some towns were devastated when their battalion was annihilated. It has even been argued that 1 July 1916 changed the face of British society more comprehensively than any other event in history.

Despite the losses, the British continued to launch smaller attacks; on 13 July the German second line was penetrated briefly, and on 15 September further ground was gained by the first attack of 'land-ships' (tanks), marking the beginning of armoured warfare, at Flers, but their use was premature and the attack was halted. By the end of November only about eight miles had been gained, at a cost of about 420,000 British and almost 200,000 French casualties; yet though the losses were manifestly not worth the result, it had relieved pressure on Verdun which might otherwise have fallen, and the continuous German counter-attacks had cost them about 650,000 men, including the cream of the officers and NCOs. Among the most terrible battles in history, the Somme had destroyed the best elements of both the British and German armies.

24 April: Not directly part of the war but arising from it was the brief but violent 'Easter Rising' of Irish nationalists in Dublin; it was suppressed by the British Army after some heavy fighting.

The Eastern Front

March: Attempting to divert German resources from the Western Front, the Russians launched an attack on 18 March in the Lake Naroch—Vilna area, but it foundered amid the mud of the spring thaw; it cost about 100,000 Russian casualties and about one-fifth that number of Germans.

4 June: With Italy under pressure from Austria, a second Russian advance was made by General Alexei Brusilov of the South-Western Army Group. Attacking on a front of 300 miles, the 'Brusilov Offensive' took the Austro-Germans by surprise, breaking their defences in two places and temporarily almost destroying the Austrian IV Army. Brusilov's troops were largely unsupported by the other Russian forces on the Eastern Front, allowing a German counter-attack to stop the Russian advance towards the north.

16 June—early August: The German counter-attack stabilized the line until Brusilov made a second drive from 28 July, pushing the defenders further back.

7 August—20 September: Brusilov attacked again and reached the foothills of the Carpathians, until Russian exhaustion and German reinforcements rushed from the Western Front stopped the Russian advance. The Brusilov Offensive was of major consequence, drawing in resources from the Central Powers' efforts on the Western and Isonzo Fronts, devastating the Austrian Army to such a degree that but for German reinforcements its collapse might have been total, and helping to cause the dismissal of the German chief-of-staff, Erich von Falkenhayn; but despite its being Russia's most successful operation of the war, the million casualties sustained contributed to the unrest which was to result in the Revolution in the following year.

27 August: Emboldened by the success of Brusilov, Roumania finally entered the war on the Allied side after much negotiation; the Austrian territory of Transylvania was invaded immediately.

August–November: Demoted to army commander, Falkenhayn stopped the Roumanian advance with the German Ninth Army, while the Bulgarian Danube Army (with German support and under the command of the German General Mackensen) attacked the Roumanians from the south.

December: The Roumanian commander Averescu, assailed by both enemy armies (which ultimately linked) and without the Russian support he required, was defeated at the River Arges (1–4 December), Bucharest was captured (6 December) and the Roumanian forces retired into Russia, with most of the country (including its oil fields and important agricultural areas) remaining in the hands of the Central Powers. Despite the Russian successes of the Brusilov Offensive, the year ended with the Central Powers in a not disadvantageous position on the Eastern Front.

The Isonzo Front

March: Italian–Austrian combat continued to lack a decisive outcome, the Italian offensive in the fifth battle of the Isonzo (11–29 March) having no more success than its predecessors.

May–June: An Austrian surprise attack from 15 May in the Trentino area broke the Italian defences, but a counter-attack and the withdrawal of Austrian units to the threatened Eastern Front recovered some of the lost territory, though Italian losses were almost twice those of the Austrians.

August: Taking advantage of the Austrian concentration for the Trentino offensive, the Italians attacked again in the sixth battle of the Isonzo (6–17 August), but it had little more effect than the previous offensives.

September–December: Renewed Italian assaults in the seventh (14–26 September), eighth (10–12 October) and ninth (1–14 November) battles of the Isonzo achieved little except to deplete the Austrian defensive capability, so that the situation at the end of the year was little changed from that at the beginning.

The Salonika Front

1915 ended with the Allies holding a bridgehead around Salonika, the Allied forces in the area being principally French and British since the withdrawal of the Serbian Army in 1915 and the crushing of Montenegro which was forced to surrender on 25 January 1916. After re-equipping, the Serbian Army rejoined the Allied forces in July and the Allies planned to break out of their positions around Salonika, but the Bulgarian-German forces, previously satisfied with a containing operation, took the offensive in August.

July–December: Independent from the main operations, an Italian force had been opposing an Austrian contingent in Albania; in November the Italians finally drove the Austrians north, enabling them to join the main Allied forces under the nominal command of the French general Maurice Sarrail (the British contingent was under its own command).

August: The Bulgarian-German offensive drove back the Allies in the Battle of Florina (17–27 August).

September–December: Sarrail's counter-attack pushed back the Central Powers, Monastir falling on 19 November, but no further progress was made, the Allies having sustained about 50,000 casualties and the Bulgarian-German forces considerably more.

The Caucasus

January–April: A Russian advance which began from Kars in early January made considerable progress, defeating the Turkish opponents at Köprukoy (18 January) and capturing Erzerum (13–16 February); a secondary movement along the Black Sea coast, supported by the Russian Navy, captured Trebizond (18 April).

May–December: A two-pronged Turkish counter-offensive was defeated, principally at Erzinjan (25 July); by the end of August fighting slackened for the winter.

The Mesopotamian Front

The advance of the British General Charles Townshend in late 1915 had ended with his withdrawal before overwhelming Turkish strength, and from 7 December his main body (less the cavalry which escaped) was besieged in Kut-al-Amara.

January–April: As Townshend's supplies ran low, continued attempts by the British and Indian armies to break through the Turkish siege-lines were unsuccessful; faced with starvation, Townshend surrendered his garrison of more than 8,000 men on 29 April.

August: A new British commander was appointed, Sir Frederick Maude; the British continued to hold their defensive positions until an overall strategy for the area had been devised.

December: It was finally decided that Maude should resume the offensive, and from mid-December he began to advance up both banks of the Tigris with more than 160,000 men, one-third British and the remainder from the Indian Army.

The Middle Eastern Front

January–August: British efforts were directed towards extending the defences of the Suez Canal into the Sinai desert, where sporadic fighting occurred when the Turks attempted to resist. Not all British resources could be devoted to this task due to a tribal insurrection by the Senussi in western Egypt, which was suppressed by March.

June: The Arab Revolt. With British and French encouragement, the Arab chieftains of the Hejaz proclaimed their independence from Turkey and a widespread guerrilla war broke out. From mid-June all Turkish lines of communication north, as far as Syria, were threatened by the fierce and mobile Arab irregulars, who received limited Allied support.

August: A Turkish attempt to attack the British in the Sinai (with German assistance and under a German commander, General von Kressenstein) was repelled at the battle of Rumani (3 August).

August–December: The British continued to advance their Sinai lines to prepare for an advance into Palestine in the following year.

The Persian Front

To relieve pressure upon the British in Mesopotamia, the limited Russian forces in Persia advanced towards Baghdad; but upon the fall of Kut-al-Amara the Turks switched many of their resources to shield the city, and after the Russian advance was beaten back at Khanikin (1 June) they retired again in the face of a Turkish counter-offensive.

On the Western Front at least, 1916 had been the most terrible year of the war to date, the combatants suffering losses which in previous ages would have been thought insupportable: it is doubtful if either the British, French or German armies ever fully recovered from the carnage of Verdun and the Somme and the loss of so many experienced personnel. Russian gains on the Eastern Front were at a price almost unbearable, the consequences of which were to become evident in the following year;

and although the Austrians were able to keep the Isonzo Front in a state of virtual stalemate, their losses in the east destroyed much of the Empire's military resource. In the war against the Turks, despite the evacuation of the Dardanelles and the disaster of Kut, the British situation was improving so that a major offensive could be contemplated in 1917.

GERMAN ARMY: ORGANIZATION

The basic German Army organization at the outbreak of war is summarized in the previous *Fotofax* title, *1914*, but as in most armies amendments were introduced as a result of the experience of combat. Infantry regimental organization was changed to maintain firepower while reducing the number of men by the increase of 'support' weapons, principally machine-guns but including grenade-projectors and mortars *(Minen-werfer)*; the crews of such 'trench artillery' were originally distributed as platoons but in September 1918 were amalgamated into a single company. The original regimental organization of three battalions of four rifle companies each, plus a 13th, machine-gun company, was amended in 1916 when the 15-gun M/G company was replaced by three 6-gun companies, so that each battalion henceforth comprised four rifle and one M/G company. From 1917 an increasing number of light machine-guns were added to each company, and in addition to the regimental M/G companies there also existed independent machine-gun *Abteilungen*, deployed virtually as artillery.

Jäger battalions originally comprised one M/G, one cyclist and four rifle companies; the bicycle companies were eventually withdrawn and a second M/G company and a *Minenwerfer* company added in August 1916.

A wartime development was the formation of *Sturmabteil-ungen* or 'storm-troops', specially trained assault units. Some of these were maintained regimentally but from late 1915 there existed independent *Sturmbataillone* of two or three infantry companies, a machine-gun and a mortar company, and a flamethrower detachment crewed by pioneers.

The majority of the cavalry units were dismounted during the war to form *Kavallerieschützen* units for use as infantry, each cavalry regiment forming one battalion of a new three-battalion unit, each battalion of four 'squadrons' (rifle companies) plus a machine-gun 'squadron'.

Field artillery originally consisted of regiments of two *Abteil-ungen* (battalions) each, each of three 6-gun batteries. During the war regiments were re-organized into three *Abteilungen* of three 4-gun batteries each, maintaining the 36 guns per regiment, with one *Abteilung* often equipped with light field howitzers, thus mixing the type of ordnance within the regiment.

GERMAN ARMY: PERSONAL WEAPONS*

After the Franco-Prussian War had proved the superiority of the French military rifle, the Germans determined to improve their standard weapon. The Small Arms Commission and the Mauser Arms Factory initially produced the Model 1871 rifle, an improvement on the French Chassepot, itself improved in 1884 (producing the Model 1871/84), and replaced it in 1888 with a smaller-bore bolt-action rifle in imitation of the French Lebel, the *Gewehr 1888*, abbreviated to 'Gew.88'. It was 7.91mm calibre and existed as a rifle with 30-inch barrel and a carbine

*Excluding machine-guns.

('Kar.88') with 18-inch barrel, the latter not equipped to take a bayonet; it incorporated the five-round Mannlicher magazine. During the First World War the Gew.88 remained in use, especially with reserve and *Landwehr* formations, never fully disappeared from service, and many were converted to accommodate the Mauser ammunition-clip.

At the outbreak of war the regulation weapon was the *Gewehr 1898* (Gew.98), designed by the Mauser factory in 1893, the principal improvements being a flush magazine (i.e., one not projecting beneath the stock), an improved clip for charger-loading and a one-piece bolt. It weighed 9lb (9lb 14oz with bayonet), retained the 7.91mm calibre and was 49.4 inches long overall (without bayonet), with a barrel-length of 29.05in. The maximum range on the adjustable backsight was 2,000 metres, and the practicable rate of fire by a trained man was between 10 and 15 rounds per minute. A significant variety was the *Karabine 1898* (Kar.98), basically the same weapon with a 24-inch barrel; it was intended for artillery and supporting services but the shorter barrel (without materially affecting performance) made it popular with infantry for trench warfare and especially with the later 'storm troops'. Another variety, confusingly styled the *1898 Karabine* (98 Kar.) was intended as a cavalry weapon, with 18in barrel; this was deemed too short and from 1909 the cavalry began to be re-equipped with the Kar.98. The Gew.98 could be fitted with telescope sights as a sniper's rifle (by 1917 three were issued to each company), with an optional down-turning bolt-handle which required a hollowing-out of the stock on the right side above the trigger to accommodate the ball-end of the bolt (as existed on the Kar.98). This *Scharfschütze* (sniper rifle) usually fired 'K' bullets (*Keru Geschlossis*) which were armour-piercing. The Gew.98 was also modified to produce the so-called *Mehrlader (Repetier-gewehr)* (repeating-rifle) which had an extra-large magazine (*Anstechmagazin*) accommodating twenty rounds in addition to the five carried in the magazine housed in the stock; but the projecting magazine made the weapon unwieldy and it was never widely used.

Automatic rifles were used in smaller numbers. The Mondragon Automatic Rifle of 7mm calibre with 10-shot magazine projecting below the stock was used principally as an aircraft weapon before the development of machine-guns adapted for aerial use. The army's main automatic weapon was the 1915 *Muskete*, as illustrated in the previous *Fotofax* title *1915*, basically a derivative of the Danish Madsen, equipped with a bipod mount and 25-round magazine; it was restricted to the *Musketen* battalions which were intended to remain behind the front line to utilize their firepower and mobility to plug any gaps in the line through which the enemy had broken. The 1915 Bergmann Automatic Rifle was used only rarely from 1916, its firepower being diluted by its tendency to overheat and jam. Even rarer was the Bergmann MP-18, a short-barrelled sub-machine-gun (the first adopted for active service), which though a successful design was introduced so late in the war that it never attained much significance.

The bayonet was used on virtually all personal firearms (even the Mondragon Automatic Rifle), the initial Gew.98 bayonet being a narrow-bladed, quill-backed weapon swelling slightly towards the point, with a 20½-inch blade, a ribbed wooden grip and a single quillon. It was modified a number of times, most notably in 1905 as the Model 1898/05, which had a much wider 14½-inch blade, again increasing in width towards the tip; the shape was such that it gave rise to the name 'butcher-knife bayonet'. Pioneer units had a version with serrated back for use as a saw, an addition seized upon by Allied propaganda which claimed it as further proof of 'Hun frightfulness'. In addition to these patterns, 'dress' bayonets existed of the same basic style but with the metal parts plated and with no provision for attachment to the rifle; they were simply ornaments for 'walking-out dress' and not even for ceremonial parades when bayonets might have to be fixed. Later in the war there existed a range of hastily produced *Ersatz* bayonets. Scabbards were normally of blackened steel, though leather was also used, as for the original 1898 pattern.

Officers and senior NCOs were armed with swords and pistols, and machine-gun crews who might find rifles an encumbrance also carried pistols, mostly of 9mm calibre, though the Walther was 6.35mm and the Mauser 7.63mm. Initially the German Army used the six-shot Model 1883 revolver of .471 calibre (and the Saxon Cavalry pattern of .433 calibre), but from 1908 the army adopted an automatic pistol as its regulation sidearm, the 9mm Parabellum, better-known by the name of a designer, Georg Luger, who developed it from the 1893 Borchardt automatic pistol, an American invention which continued to be carried by German officers even though not the official weapon. The Parabellum initially appeared in 7.65mm calibre, but from the Model 1902 was chambered for a 9mm cartridge. It contained an 8-round magazine in the grip, with a supplementary 32-round magazine which could be attached to the base of the grip; available with short and long barrels, a shoulder-stock was available to turn it into a short carbine. Though never adopted officially, an automatic which saw widespread use was the 1898 Mauser pistol of 7.63mm calibre (or re-chambered for the standard 9mm cartridge); its magazine extended below the chamber, forward of the trigger-guard, and thus its grip was narrower than that of the Parabellum, hence the nickname 'broomhandle'. The 9mm Bayard, 9mm Browning (with long and short barrels) and the 6.35mm Walther were used only in limited numbers.

Swords soon disappeared from the combat zones as their lack of use was demonstrated; cavalry swords in general were withdrawn in 1915. Artillery and train services carried a slightly curved sabre, heavy cavalry a straight-bladed *Pallasch* with triple-bar guard, and lighter regiments a slightly shorter weapon with quarter-basket hilt; infantry and other dismounted officers used the longer 1889 sword. All had metal scabbards. Lances were carried originally only by *Uhlans*, but as in many armies the weapon was extended to all regiments in 1889, the Model 1890 lance having a length (inclusive of cruciform tip) of 10 feet 6 inches, with a tubular steel shaft. It saw little combat service after the initial brief period of fluid manoeuvre early in the war.

Of all nations, Germany was the most advanced in the production of hand-grenades, so that vast stocks of hand- and rifle-grenades were available at the outbreak of war, as a result of a commission established to investigate the lessons of the Russo-Japanese War. Almost all German grenades were ignited by a time fuze, though a few percussion varieties existed, most notably the 1914-pattern Rifle Grenade, the 'disc' pattern (resembling a convex discus) and some examples of the 'stick grenade'. Though more rifle-grenades were available initially than hand-grenades, their lack of accuracy led to their decline until the manufacture of new types from 1917, discharged from a cup affixed to the rifle-muzzle with an ordinary cartridge for propellant, instead of the rod-fittings of the earlier patterns. The best-known hand-grenade was the 'stick grenade' (*Stielhand-*granate) or 'potato-masher', a metal cylinder of explosive with a hollow wooden handle protruding from the base, through which the fuze ran, ignition being caused by pulling the cord which protruded from the bottom of the handle. Another version had a solid handle and a fuze which protruded alongside the handle from the base of the cylindrical head. Other types included the spherical pattern (*Kugelhandgranate*) which was a cast-iron, 3-inch diameter segmented ball with a friction-tube inserted in the top, ignition occurring when the wire loop at the top was withdrawn; a leather wrist-loop was often attached for this purpose. The 'egg-grenade' (*Eierhandgranate*) was of similar type, but with the cast-iron body ovoid in shape; and the 'parachute grenade' had a fabric 'parachute' stabilizer attached to the bottom of the cylinder which resembled the shape of a rifle-grenade. A number of varieties of spherical gas-grenades were produced, with thin steel exteriors and containing about ⅔-pint of liquid released by the bursting-charge, but these were never very widely used. The grenade-discharger which fired a finned projectile much farther than it was possible to throw a hand-grenade was not a 'personal' weapon but, like the trench mortar, was a piece of trench artillery.

Three basic varieties of flamethrower were used by the German Army, but one (the *Grossflammenwerfer*) was static and had to be erected in a trench, and the *Kleinflammenwerfer*, though portable, was still cumbersome: it could be carried on the back of one member of the crew and its hose and nozzle directed by another. Only the much lighter *Wex* was truly a portable 'personal weapon', with the advantage of automatic ignition, whereas the others had to be ignited by a taper or match applied to the jet of flammable liquid issuing from the nozzle.

REGIMENTS OF THE GERMAN ARMY

The various regiments of the German Army were numbered consecutively irrespective of their state of origin and the fact that some states retained a degree of independence in their organization and uniform. The following list shows the 'state' composition of the army but does not attempt to give full titles; it was usual for regimental appellations to give the name of the dignitary from whom the unit took its title (if any), then the 'state' number (e.g., 1st Brandenburg) and finally their number in the line, thus: *Grenadier-Regiment König Friedrich I (4. Ostpreussisches) Nr. 5*. The units which comprised the German Army were as follows:

Prussian Guard
1st–5th Foot Guards; 1st–5th Guard Grenadiers; Fusiliers; *Jägers*; *Schützen* (Sharpshooters).

Infantry: Grenadiers
Line regiments numbered: 1 (1st E. Prussian), 2 (1st Pomeranian), 3–5 (2nd–4th E. Prussian), 6–7 (1st–2nd W. Prussian), 8 (1st Brandenburg Leib-Grenadiers), 9 (2nd Pomeranian: Colberg Grenadiers), 10–11 (1st–2nd Silesian), 12 (2nd Brandenburg), 89 (Mecklenburg), 100 (1st Saxon Leib-Grenadiers), 101 (2nd Saxon), 109 (1st Baden Leib-Grenadiers), 110 (2nd Baden), 119 (1st Württemberg).

Infantry: Fusiliers
Line regiments numbered: 33 (E. Prussian), 34 (Pomeranian), 35 (Brandenburg), 36 (Magdeburg), 37 (Westphalian), 38

(Silesian), 39 (Lower Rhenish), 40 (Hohenzollern), 73 (Hanoverian), 80 (Hessian), 86 (Schleswig-Holstein), 90 (Mecklenburg), 108 (Saxon), 122 (4th Württemberg).

Infantry: line regiments
Regiments numbered: 13, 15–17, 53, 55–57 (1st–8th Westphalian); 14, 21, 42, 49, 54, 61 (1st–8th Pomeranian); 18–19, 58–59 (1st–4th Posen); 20, 24, 48, 52, 60, 64 (3rd–8th Brandenburg); 22–23, 62–63 (1st–4th Upper Silesian); 25, 28–30, 65, 68–70, 160–61 (1st–10th Rhenish); 26–27, 66–67 (1st–4th Magdeburg); 31–32, 71–72, 94–96, 153 (1st–8th Thuringian); 41, 43–45 (5th–8th E. Prussian); 46–47, 50–51, 154 (1st–5th Lower Silesian); 74, 77–78, 164–65 (1st–5th Hanoverian); 75–76 (1st–2nd Hanseatic); 78 (E. Frisian); 81–83 (1st–3rd Hessian); 84 (Schleswig); 85 (Holstein); 87–88 (1st–2nd Nassau); 91 (Oldenburg); 92 (Brunswick); 93 (Anhalt); 97, 99 (1st–2nd Oberheim); 98 (Metz); 102–07, 133–34, 139, 177–79, 181 (3rd–15th Saxon); 111–14, 142, 169–70 (3rd–9th Baden); 115 (1st Hessian Grand-Ducal *Leibgarde*); 116–18, 168 (2nd–5th Hessian Grand-Ducal); 120, 123–27, 180 (2nd, 5th–8th Württemberg); 121 (Old Württemberg); 128 (Danzig); 129, 140, 148–49, 155, 175–76 (3rd–9th W. Prussian); 130–131, 135–36, 144–45, 156–57, 173–74 (1st–10th Lorraine); 132, 137–38, 143 (1st–4th Lower Alsace); 141 (Kulmer); 146–47 (1st–2nd Masuria); 150–51 (1st–2nd Ermland); 152 (Deutsch–Ordens); 156–57 (3rd–4th Silesian); 162 (Lübeck, 3rd Hanseatic); 163 (Schleswig-Holstein); 166 (Hesse-Homburg); 167, 171–72 (1st–3rd Upper Alsace).

Jägers
Battalions numbered: 1 (E. Prussian), 2 (Pomeranian), 3 (Brandenburg), 4 (Magdeburg), 5–6 (1st–2nd Silesian), 7 (Westphalian), 8 (Rhenish), 9 (Laurenberg), 10 (Hanoverian), 11 (Hessian), 12–13 (1st–2nd Saxon), 14 (Mecklenburg).

Cavalry: Prussian Guard
Garde du Corps, Guard Cuirassiers, 1st–2nd Dragoons, Guard Hussars, 1st–3rd *Uhlans*.

Cavalry: Saxon heavy regiments
Saxon Guard Regiment, Saxon Carabiniers.

Cavalry: Cuirassiers
Regiments numbered: 1 (Silesian), 2 (Pomeranian), 3 (E. Prussian), 4 (Westphalian), 5 (W. Prussian), 6 (Brandenburg), 7 (Magdeburg), 8 (Rhenish).

Cavalry: Dragoons
Regiments numbered: 1 (Lithuanian), 2, 12 (1st–2nd Brandenburg), 3 (Neumark), 4, 8, 15 (1st–3rd Silesian), 5 (Rhenish), 6 (Magdeburg), 7 (Westphalian), 9, 16 (1st–2nd Hanoverian), 10 (E. Prussian), 11 (Pomeranian), 13 (Schleswig-Holstein), 14 (Kurmark), 17, 18 (1st–2nd Mecklenburg), 19 (Oldenburg), 20–22 (1st–3rd Baden), 23 (Hessian Guard), 24 (2nd Hessian), 25–26 (1st–2nd Württemberg).

Cavalry: Hussars
Regiments numbered: 1–2 (1st–2nd Leib-Hussars), 3 (Brandenburg), 4, 6 (1st–2nd Silesian), 5 (Pomeranian), 7, 9

(1st–2nd Rhenish), 8, 11 (1st–2nd Westphalian), 10 (Magdeburg), 12 (Thuringian), 13–14 (1st–2nd Hessian), 15 (Hanoverian), 16 (Schleswig-Holstein), 17 (Brunswick), 18–19 (1st–2nd Saxon).

Cavalry: Uhlans
Regiments numbered: 1 (W. Prussian), 2 (Silesian), 3, 11 (1st–2nd Brandenburg), 4, 9 (1st–2nd Pomeranian), 5 (Westphalian), 6 (Thuringian), 7 (Rhenish), 8 (E. Prussian), 10 (Posen), 12 (Lithuanian), 13–14 (1st–2nd Hanoverian), 15 (Schleswig-Holstein), 16 (Altmark), 17, 18, 21 (1st–3rd Saxon), 19–20 (1st–2nd Württemberg).

Field Artillery
1st–4th (Prussian) Guard; regiments numbered: 1 (Prince August of Prussia's); 2, 17 (1st–2nd Pomeranian); 3, 18 (1st–2nd Brandenburg); 4 (Magdeburg); 5, 41 (1st–2nd Lower Silesian); 6, 42 (1st–2nd Silesian); 7, 22 (1st–2nd Westphalian); 8, 23 (1st–2nd Rhenish); 9 (Schleswig); 10, 26 (1st–2nd Hanoverian); 11, 25, 47, 61 (Hessian); 12, 28, 32, 48, 64, 68, 77, 78 (1st–8th Saxon); 13, 29, 49, 65 (1st–4th Württemberg); 14, 30, 50, 76 (1st–5th Baden); 15, 51 (1st–2nd Upper Alsace); 16, 52 (1st–2nd E. Prussian); 19, 55 (1st–2nd Thuringian); 20, 56 (1st–2nd Posen); 21, 57 (1st–2nd Upper Silesian); 24 (Holstein); 27, 63 (1st–2nd Nassau); 31, 67 1st–2nd (Lower Alsace); 33, 34, 69, 70 (1st–4th Lorraine); 35, 36 (1st–2nd W. Prussian); 37 (Lithuanian); 38 (Upper Pomeranian); 39 (Kurmark); 40 (Altmark); 43 (Cleves); 44 (Treves); 45 (Laurenburg); 46 (Lower Saxon); 53 (Lower Pomeranian); 54 (Neumark); 58 (Minden); 59 (Berg); 60 (Mecklenburg); 62 (Ostfries); 71 (Komthur); 72 (Hochmeister); 73 (Masuria); 74 (Torgau); 75 (Mansfeld).

Foot Artillery
Guard Regiment; line regiments 1, 2, 4, 6 with 'personal' titles; 3 (Brandenburg), 5 (Lower Silesian), 7 (Westphalian), 8 (Rhenish), 9 (Schleswig-Holstein), 10 (Lower Saxony), 11, 15 (1st–2nd W. Prussian), 12 (Saxon), 13 (Hohenzollern), 14 (Baden).

Pioneers
Guard Battalion; line battalions numbered: 1 (E. Prussian), 2 (Pomeranian), 3 (Brandenburg), 4 (Magdeburg), 5 (Lower Silesian), 6 (Silesian), 7 (Westphalian), 8 (Rhenish), 9 (Schleswig-Holstein), 10 (Hanoverian), 11 (Hessian), 12, 22 (1st–2nd Saxon), 13 (Württemberg), 14 (Baden), 15, 19 1st–2nd Alsace), 16, 20 (1st–2nd Lorraine), 17, 23 (1st–2nd W. Prussian), 18 (Samland), 21 (Nassau).

Train
Guard Battalion, and 19 line battalions bearing the same state designations as Pioneer battalions with the same number, except: 18 (Hessian Grand-Ducal); 19 (2nd Saxon).

Bavarian Army (remained independent of the numbering of the remainder of the German Army)
Infantry: Leib-Regiment; 1st–23rd Infantry; 1st–2nd *Jägers*.
Cavalry: 1st–2nd Heavy Cavalry; 1st–2nd *Uhlans*; 1st–7th *Chevaulegers*.
Artillery: 1st–12th Field Regiments, 1st–2nd Foot Regiments.
Supports: 1st–3rd Pioneer Battalions, 1st–3rd Train Battalions.

SOURCES AND BIBLIOGRAPHY

Although this lists works applicable to the war as a whole, as noted in the earlier titles *1914* and *1915*, emphasis is given to the actions of 1916 and to the German Army which figures in the data section.

Barker, A. J. *The Neglected War: Mesopotamia 1914–18.* London, 1967

Chappell, M. *British Battle Insignia 1914–18.* London, 1986
— *The British Soldier in the 20th Century.* Hatherleigh (series) from 1987

Farrar-Hockley, A. H. *The Somme.* London, 1964

Fosten, D. S. V., and Marrion, R. J. *The German Army 1914–18.* London, 1978

Hicks, J. E. *French Military Weapons.* New Milford, Connecticut, 1964
— *German Weapons, Uniforms, Insignia 1841–1918.* La Canada, California, 1958

Horne, A. *The Price of Glory: Verdun 1916.* London, 1962

Laffin, J. *Western Front 1916–17: the Price of Honour.* Sydney, 1987

Middlebrook, M. *The First Day on the Somme.* London, 1971

Mollo, A. *Army Uniforms of World War I.* Poole, 1977 (the most outstanding modern work on the subject)

Nash, D. B. *German Infantry 1914–18.* London, 1977
— *Imperial German Army Handbook 1914–18.* London, 1980

Nash, D. B. (ed.) *German Army Handbook 1918.* London, 1977

Nicolle, D. *Lawrence and the Arab Revolt.* London, 1989

Rankin, R. H. *Helmets and Headdress of the Imperial German Army 1870–1918.* New Milford, Connecticut, 1965

Walter, A. (ed.) *Guns of the First World War.* London, 1988 (a reprint of the *Text Book of Small Arms*, 1909)

Wilson, H. W. (ed.) *The Great War.* London, 1916 (contemporary periodical containing much significant photography and artwork)

An important article especially relevant to the modification of uniforms on campaign, concerning the Lancashire Fusiliers on the Somme, by M. Chappell, appeared in the periodical *Military Illustrated*, No. 1, London, 1986.

46. ANZACs on the march on the Western Front. Although motor transport was used increasingly during the war, horse-drawn vehicles and light carts pulled manually remained in use. The troops illustrated are unmistakably New Zealanders, their slouch hats being pinched up into the four-cornered crown like the hats worn by Boy Scouts and by the US Army.

46 ▼

▲47

▲48 ▼49

47. Though British Empire forces were equipped in British style, a number of distinctive patterns existed. This is an excellent depiction of the Australian tunic, made in drab or khaki serge, flannel or cord, which after exposure to the elements often faded to its natural blue-grey shade. The equipment is like that of the British 1908 pattern, but may include leather cartridge-pouches; the slouch hat, jealously guarded throughout the war, was the most characteristic item of Australian uniform. This 'Digger's' two attractive companions are South African recruiters, photographed on an Australian visit to Durban en route to the war. Their pseudo-military uniform was calculated to attract volunteers to the enlistment-booths!

48. Perhaps the most bizarre item of equipment devised during the period was the Canadian 'tump-line' device, a webbing strap which took some of the weight off the soldier's back by supporting it on his head, a method of weight-distribution used in the wilds of north-west Canada. It was designed by Captain Archibald who had won the high jump at the London Olympics, but not surprisingly it had only a very limited use!

49. A Belgian makes a sandwich in the entrance to his dug-out in the Belgian sector of the Western Front, from Ypres to the sea. The 1915-pattern Belgian uniform was produced in khaki because Britain could supply the cloth, but was basically in French style and included the Adrian helmet, painted khaki, with an embossed lion-mask badge on the front. This man has a fabric cover over his helmet and a double-breasted greatcoat; khaki trousers were worn with matching puttees or leather ankle-gaiters. The equipment hanging by the door of the dug-out is the 1915 pattern in brown leather; British-style webbing was manufactured later. Note the trench construction,

combining ancient-style gabions and chicken-wire.

50. A Belgian trench-mortar gunner wearing the 1915-pattern khaki tunic, trousers and puttees, with ankle-boots and khaki-painted Adrian helmet. For the artillery the collar-patch was royal blue with scarlet piping, and scarlet-piped shoulder-straps. Similarly, other branches had distinctive colours: infantry scarlet patch and royal blue piping; light infantry green patch and yellow piping; engineers black patch and scarlet piping, etc. The weapon is the French '58 cal' No. 2 mortar with finned bomb; range was varied by elevation or depression of the barrel on the slide illustrated.

51. Although some Indian Army units remained on the Western Front throughout the war, much of the army's effort was concentrated in Mesopotamia and, in the case of the Gurkhas, in the Dardanelles. This depicts the pipers of an unidentified Gurkha battalion entertaining French civilians; both pipers and spectators wear knitted woollen caps in place of their

more characteristic slouch hats. These indomitable Nepalese soldiers were thoroughly feared

by all enemies who experienced their kukri-swinging charge and war-cry '*Ayo Gurkhali!*'

50▲

51▼

52. *Generalfeldmarschall* Paul Ludwig von Beneckendorf und von Hindenburg (1874–1934) and his chief-of-staff Erich von Ludendorff (1865–1937) had commanded on the Eastern Front with considerable success until appointed to overall command on the Western Front after the admissal of von Falkenheyn in August 1916. General officers' uniform included a gold-embroidered fringed loop decoration on a red collar-patch, but in typical style Hindenburg apparently wears the regimental uniform of the 3rd Foot Guards, with *Garde-Litzen* on the collar-patch. His grey greatcoat had scarlet lapels and piping on the upper edge of the cuff, and gold and silver braid shoulder-straps on red backing, bearing the silver crossed batons of field marshal's rank; the cap had scarlet band and piping. Hindenburg served as president of the republic from 1925 to 1934, latterly (reluctantly) accepting Hitler as chancellor; Ludendorff, a far less noble character, adopted extreme nationalism and marched with Hitler in the abortive Munich *putsch*.

53. The French *Soixante-quinze* (75mm) fieldpiece was probably the most famous ordnance of the war, but earlier models remained in use. This gun-position in the Argonne has a Modèle 1877 'Système de Bange' of which the 80mm and 90mm calibre were normally employed in the field, but this is a larger 120L variety originally intended for siege and garrison use. Note the plates attached to the wheels (*ceintures de roues*) and ramps positioned behind the wheels to absorb the recoil of firing and prevent the gun from having to be re-positioned totally after each shot.

54. The Allied armies on the Western Front maintained considerable mounted forces in the hope that they might be able to exploit the breakthrough that never came. Among the most anachronistic were the French Spahis, the near-legendary north African cavalry who retained their singular

53 ▲   54 ▼

equipment even when serving in Europe: this rear view illustrates the high-backed saddle (not dissimilar to the European 'great saddle' of the 17th century) and the flowing cloak, the oriental appearance somewhat marred by the steel helmet (which for African colonial troops bore a frontal badge of 'RF' within a crescent). The carbine slung on the back is the 8mm Model 1890.

▲55

▲56

55. Among the best units of the French Army were the Algerian and Tunisian *Tirailleurs*. Their designations could be confusing: they were often referred to by initials, R.M.T. (*Régiment de Marche de Tirailleurs*), R.T.A. (*Régiment des Tirailleurs Algériens*), or R.M.Z.T. (*Régiment mixte de Zouaves et de Tirailleurs*).

Uniform included the 'native' *chéchia* cap and khaki clothing, though other colours were pressed into service, such as 'horizon blue' greatcoats and even uniforms of the khaki shade styled *tenue réséda* originally intended for the Greek army. The *chéchias* here bear star-and-crescent insignia, but on campaign were usually concealed by a horizon blue cover, until the issue of the Adrian helmet, originally blue but repainted khaki as soon as possible.

56. Among the most unusual uniforms seen in Europe was that of the French Annamite infantry, part of the garrison of Cochin-China sent to the main theatre of war. Their uniform was khaki like that of other colonial corps, but included the unique straw or bamboo-fibre hat covered with grey cloth; for active service in Europe these were replaced by berets of the style worn by the *Chasseurs Alpins*. They served both in France and at Salonika.

▼57

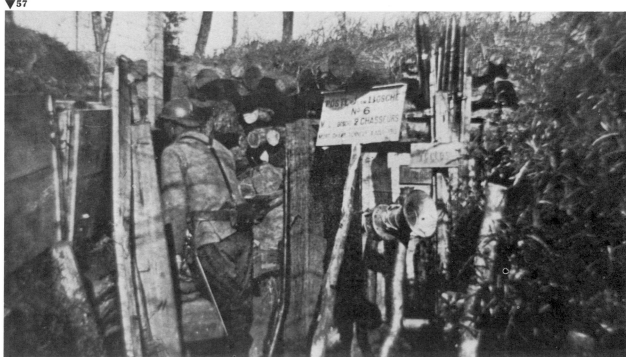

57. A French listening-post on the Aisne. The sentry is using a trench periscope; note the klaxon to warn of gas attack, and the sheaf of rockets to signal for support. This demonstrates a notable difference between the systems of naming trenches and posts: whereas the British used homely names often taken from the home areas of the troops involved ('Pendle Hill Street', 'Sauchiehall Street', etc), this French post is named after a fallen hero, Jean Bosche of the 2nd *Chasseurs*, with the immortal phrase on the name-board, '*Mort au Champ d'Honneur*', 4 August 1915.

58. The Irish 'Easter Rising' of 1916 was not properly part of the war, but took advantage of British preoccupation; heavy fighting occurred in Dublin before the rising was crushed. This remarkable British armoured vehicle was made in the yard of the Guinness brewery from a number of railway-engine smoke-boxes

mounted on a flat lorry, with an engine-cab at the rear to protect the driver. It was loopholed to enable the crew inside to return fire with little danger of being hit in return.

59. Easily transportable light machine-guns were adopted by most armies by the middle of the war; weapons like the French Chauchat and the Madsen derivative with which the German *Muskete* battalions were armed allowed infantry to possess their own fire-support without having to rely on the heavier machine-guns. The American-designed .303 calibre Lewis gun was adopted by the British Army from 1915; weighing 26lb, it was air-cooled with an aluminium barrel-casing and a drum magazine on top, capable of 550 rounds per minute, and was operated by one man. It is shown here on an anti-aircraft mounting on a car; normally it had a small bipod mount. A spare magazine is held by the man in the background.

60. Mechanized transport was first used to a considerable extent during the war; the first military transports were requisitioned civilian vehicles, but by 1916 specially designed transport was universal. This example crewed by members of the Royal Flying Corps is a Leyland 3-ton S-type lorry with the later pattern steel disc wheels instead of the original

▼62

cast-iron spoked variety. In this photograph the canvas tilt over the cab has been folded back. Note the use of the webbing waist-belt with the RFC khaki 'maternity jacket' (extreme right).

61. Although the British Royal Flying Corps had a prescribed uniform, officers serving on attachment usually retained their regimental uniform. In this photograph of probably Britain's most famous 'ace', Lieutenant (Temporary Captain) Albert Ball wears the uniform of his 7th (Robin Hood) Battalion, Sherwood Foresters (Nottinghamshire and Derbyshire Regiment) with the bronzed regimental collar-badges, with only the goggles suggesting his attachment to the RFC. The first man to win the Distinguished Service Order three times, Ball was a shy Nottingham youth who became one of the most intrepid fighter-pilots of the war; after his death in action at the age of 20 on 7 May 1917 he was awarded a Victoria Cross.

62. The regulation uniform of the Royal Flying Corps was the khaki 'maternity jacket', cavalry-style side-cap, trousers and puttees. This group of senior NCOs includes a number of 'active service' variations, including the use of long woollen stockings in place of puttees (central figure). Flight-Sergeant W. H. Duckworth (seated left) purchased his own uniform which was tailored privately, here without shoulder-titles and including cavalry riding-breeches and leather 'Stohwasser' cavalry leggings.

63. The Tsar (left) and General Alexeevich Brusilov (1853–1926), architect of the 'Brusilov offensive', who made his name in the 1877–8 Russo-Turkish War and in 1916 proved himself the most capable Russian general of the war; in 1917 he joined the Soviets but was not actively employed again. Both wear the officers' version of the khaki greatcoat with rigid shoulder-boards and scarlet collar-patch, khaki breeches with scarlet stripes, and khaki cap; both carry the 1909-pattern sword (uniquely the Russians carried them with the hilt towards the rear) on a brown leather belt.

64. Although the United States did not enter the war until 1917, many individuals served in the armies of other states. Russia's long history of the employment of foreign officers is demonstrated by this photograph of Dr P. Newton, who took to Russia a Field Ambulance corps paid for by American sympathisers. He wears the officers' uniform of the Russian army: khaki peaked cap with domed oval cockade with 'sunburst' edging, and a khaki tunic with standing collar and pointed breast- and side-pockets. The conspicuous rigid shoulder-boards covered with metallic lace and bearing rank-stars were often replaced on campaign by soft shoulder-straps with khaki rank-lace, or plain shoulder-straps with the insignia drawn or stencilled on.

63 ▲   64 ▼

65. A Russian gun-team on the Eastern Front, including a youthful cadet. The grey-brown double-breasted greatcoat had a falling collar bearing a patch in the service colour (black with red piping for artillery), and the usual double-sided shoulder-straps: one side in the facing-colour (artillery red) and the other in the garment-colour with (for rank-and-file) crossed cannon-barrels and the brigade number stencilled in red. The NCO in the centre, wearing the Cross of St. George, appears to have the wide gold stripe across the top of the shoulder-strap indicative of sergeant's rank. The cadet is armed with cossack-style artillery *Shashqa*, the guard-less sabre shorter than the cavalry pattern.

66. Russian troops queue for a hair-cut by electric clippers powered by hand-cranked generator. They wear the grey-brown greatcoat with collar-patch in the service colour: black piped red for artillery and engineers, green piped red for rifle corps, and red, blue, white or green respectively for the 1st-4th regiments in each infantry division. Shoulder-straps were red for Guards, artillery, engineers and the 1st and 2nd regiments in each line division, blue for the 3rd and 4th, crimson for rifle corps and yellow for grenadier divisions; on service they were usually reversed to show khaki with badge or regimental number usually in red for artillery, yellow for infantry and brown for engineer services. The third man in the queue appears to have a coloured strap bearing the single metallic lace stripe of sergeants' rank.

67. Some images from the war are uncannily like those of a previous age: this photograph might appear to depict a scene from Napoleon's retreat from Moscow, but in fact shows a Cossack patrol in the Caucasus. Although the Steppe Cossacks (the larger group) wore a version of the standard army uniform, the Caucasian Cossacks (Kuban and Terek) retained a 'native' costume of grey or black astrakhan cap,

▲65 ▼66

▼67

black or dark-grey kaftan (*Cherkeska*) with cartridge- tubes at each side of the breast, red shoulder-straps and collar- patch for Kuban and blue for Terek units.

68. Like the aviation services of most nations, that of the Russian forces was part of the army, trained and equipped by France. These officers affixing a bomb wear the distinctive uniform of the service, a black side-cap with red piping and silver-laced crown, dark blue shirt and red-piped black breeches, though the usual flying-dress included a leather helmet and black leather jacket. The shoulder-boards here show clearly the rank-marking of company officers: metallic lace straps with a central stripe of arm-of-service colour, with up to three stars.

69. Despite the Russians' pressing need for troops and *matériel*, they demonstrated solidarity with their allies by sending contingents to fight on the Western Front and to Salonika. They retained their national uniform, but those serving alongside the French adopted the ubiquitous *casque Adrian*. The Russian rifle was the 1891-pattern Mosin-Nagant (also known as the '3-line' or sometimes 1900-pattern even through basically identical with the 1891), a charger-loading 7.62mm calibre weapon, but to facilitate ammunition supply the Russians in France carried the French Lebel rifle.

70. An Italian infantry unit on the march, headed by the machine-gun section carrying the guns, barrels and mountings separately, on the backs of the crew. The 1909 grey-green uniform had padded rolls on the shoulders (to prevent the equipment slipping), matching trousers and puttees, and collar-patches coloured according to the branch: crimson for infantry; for machine-gunners they were pointed-ended with white stripes, blue, green and red respectively for the teams of St-Etienne, Maxim and Fiat guns. The wide black chevrons above the cuffs are the rank-insignia of senior privates (equating with lance-corporals in the British Army, for example). A black machine-gun badge was worn on the left sleeve.

68▲ 69▼

70▼

71. An Italian light fieldpiece firing from a turf embrasure on the Italian Front. The crew wear the 1909 grey-green uniform, which for artillery had a black 'flame'-pointed collar-patch piped yellow; the field-cap bore an embroidered yellow grenade over crossed cannon-barrels, later produced in less visible black embroidery. The officers (as in right foreground, wearing leather gaiters instead of the grey-green puttees of the other ranks) had rank-insignia of one to three stars (for company officers) on the shoulder-straps, and a similar number of metallic lace bands on the cap, later changed to less visible yellow or grey lace. Note the ramps positioned behind the gun-wheels to prevent excessive recoil

72. Italian sentries manning a trench on the Italian Front in about August 1916. By now the Italian Army had adopted the French Adrian helmet, but of superior construction and without the embossed metal badge on the front as used by most nations which adopted the pattern; instead, Italian regimental insignia was often stencilled on in black paint, for infantry (for example) a crowned regimental number, backed by crossed rifles for NCOs and above. Personal equipment was produced in grey-green leather, matching the uniform-colour, with four ammunition-pouches for dismounted personnel. The rifle was the 1891-pattern 6.5mm Mannlicher-Carcano, taking a 6-round clip, though large quantities of earlier 6.5mm Vetterli rifles remained in use.

73. Italy's 6-inch 'position' guns fulfilled a similar role to the famous French '75', because despite firing a heavy shell with long range they were comparatively light and easy to transport. The gun here, en route to the Italian Front, has 'caterpillars' attached to the wheels to facilitate movement over rough or soft ground. Italian mounted troops like this

artillery driver wore a tunic like
that of the infantry but with
shoulder-straps instead of 'rolls'
at the point of the shoulder,
grey-green riding-breeches,
black leather gaiters and
spurred ankle-boots instead of
puttees.

74. A rapid mode of
constructing trenches in
mountainous terrain, as in the
Alps: wire-netting baskets filled
with sandbags. These Austrian
machine-gunners apparently
wear the 1909 pike-grey
(*Hechtgrau*) field uniform with
soft cap, though from 1915 a
new uniform began to come
into use, similar to the previous
pattern but in field-grey, with a
steel helmet initially of German
pattern but later with a flatter
lower edge, often styled a
'Berndorfer' helmet after its
designer. Until 1917 regimental
identity was indicated by the
colour of collar-patch and
buttons; the man at the right
appears to have the two stars on
the collar indicative of
corporals' rank.

75. A number of armies had ski-
borne infantry, the French
Chasseurs Alpins being perhaps
the most famous. This Austrian
unit in the Alps appears to wear
the pike-grey infantry uniform,
most with the trousers with
integral gaiters instead of the
breeches and long stockings of
the *Landesschützen* mountain
troops, but the pile of
equipment at the right appears
to consist of rucksacks as
carried by the latter, instead of
the ordinary infantry pack. The
piled rifles are apparently the
1895 8mm Mannlicher, a clip-
loading weapon 50 inches long,
rather than the 1895 short
carbine of the *Landesschützen*.

73▲   74▼

75▼

▲76 ▼77

▼78

77. Muddy roads were endemic not only on the Western Front but equally in the East. Here in Serbia a German staff-car is bogged to its running-boards despite the efforts of the officers endeavouring to push it free.

76. Although some units had been trained in mountain warfare earlier, the first German ski-corps were formed in 1915, the 1st–4th Bavarian Ski Battalions (*Schneeschuh-Bataillon*). The Württemberg *Gebirgs- und Schneeschuh Bataillon* was formed in October 1915 and served in the Vosges, in Roumania and on the Italian Front, being expanded to regimental strength in 1918. Their grey uniform had a black collar-patch bearing a green letter 'S' (*Schützen*: rifles) and small green shoulder-rolls; the peaked field-cap was similar to Austrian style. Equipment and arms were of infantry pattern, with rucksack instead of pack, and white and camouflaged hooded snow-suits were also used.

79▲

80▲   81▼

Note the rear skirts of the 1910 tunic of the central figure, showing the false pockets each with three buttons and coloured piping. A slower but more reliable method of transport is visible at the right: ox-carts were used by all combatants in the region, and oxen were even used for hauling artillery.

78. The uniform of the Roumanian Army is illustrated in this portrait of General I. Culcer, commanding their First Army. From 1912 a grey-green field uniform was introduced, with a field-cap bearing the red, yellow and blue national cockade and piping in the arm-of-service colour for officers; a fly-fronted tunic with breast- and side-pockets in grey-green with standing colour bearing the collar-patch (red for generals, as here, and infantry); grey-green breeches (black for artillery and cavalry); and black riding-boots or brown ankle-boots and gaiters. Rank was indicated by the shoulder-strap device, here gold lace straps piped red, with three silver stars. From May 1916 a uniform of French manufacture in 'horizon blue' was authorized, but except for a number of officers it was not widely used.

79. After evacuation from its homeland, the Serbian Army was re-equipped in 1916 by the Allied nations, partly in British khaki and partly in French 'horizon blue', including the Adrian steel helmet. This depicts a cavalry unit equipped and serving as infantry at Salonika, with French-style uniform and equipment. The Adrian helmet bore an embossed metal badge on the front of the Serbian arms, a double eagle with a shield bearing a cross upon its breast, as on the standard carried here.

80. Casualty evacuation in the Salonika area utilizing a 'mule cacolet', a harness with a seat on each side to enable less severely wounded men to ride over rough country. Two Highlanders form the mule's burden; the 2nd Battalion, Camerons and 1st Battalion, Argyll and Sutherland were both with the 27th Division at Salonika from December 1915. The white labels attached to their breast-pockets would give details of injury and treatment given at the advanced dressing-station.

81. This sergeant with the rather severe haircut is using a trench periscope at Salonika, the upper part camouflaged with fabric. His unit is identified by the brass shoulder-title 'Y & L': 1st Battalion, York and Lancaster Regiment, which arrived in Salonika in early December 1915 as part of 83 Brigade, 28th Division, in which theatre it served for the remainder of the war.

▲82 ▼83

▲84

82. Prior to formation of the British Army's Corps of Signals in 1920, communications were the responsibiity of the Royal Engineers' 'signal service'. This officer operating a field-telephone at Salonika wears the white over blue 'armlet' or brassard on both upper sleeves which identified signals personnel. Rank-insignia is carried on the shoulder-strap, much less visible than on the cuff; the Sam Browne belt is worn with double shoulder-braces. The pistol by the officer's right hand is a Mauser automatic, perhaps captured

from the Germans, though such weapons were also available in Britain for private purchase before the war. The man behind the officer has the ordinary brass 'RE' shoulder-titles, without the additional 'Signal Service' title underneath.

83. Although 19th-century mortars had been pressed into service by the French at the beginning of the war, 'trench artillery' was soon designed to enable infantry to have close-range artillery support, trench mortars lobbing bombs over a limited range. The German

▼85

Minenwerfer was probably the most effective, the bombs dropping with a whine (hence the British nickname 'moaning minnie'; 'minnie' = *Minenwerfer*), but all operated on a similar principle, having a flat base-plate to absorb recoil. This British officer at Salonika is somewhat gingerly about to fire a British 'Tock Emma' (T/M: trench mortar).

84. Among the most unusual items of uniform in the European theatres of war were sun-hats, both of the Australian-style 'slouch' pattern and others of more bizarre shape. This group of engineers (including some French personnel) shows British Royal Engineers in a variety of sun-hats; the location is unknown but may be Macedonia, where such head-dress was quite common with the British forces.

85. The uniform of the British forces in Mesopotamia (alias 'Mespot'!) was like that worn in India, khaki drill with topees. The heat led to the addition of other sunshades, such as the huge quilted neck-shade fastened around the topee in this photograph. The soldier illustrated has improvised a feeding-bottle for milk with which to feed this tiny gazelle, a wonderfully humanitarian scene from a bitter war.

86. Medical inspection of an Indian Mountain Battery at Salonika. The uniforms are like those worn in India despite being in a European theatre: British officers continued to wear tropical helmets (as indeed did some British units even in Italy) and khaki drill. The medical officer here wears rank-insignia on the shoulder-straps, a style eventually also seen on the Western Front, being less distinct to enemy snipers than the large rank-badges on the cuff; the crown on the shoulder-strap identifies his rank as that of major, the metal title 'IMS' indicating 'Indian Medical Service'.

87. Roll-call of an Indian infantry company in Mesopotamia. The Mesopotamian campaign was administered largely by the Indian Army, which provided the majority of the troops involved. Note here the 1903 leather bandolier equipment; unlike most of the Empire or Dominion troops, the Indian Army did not receive the 1908 web equipment until 1921. Calling the roll is an Indian commissioned officer, wearing an empty sword-frog on the waist-belt. The British officer wears a typical uniform, including shorts, the use of which eventually spread to the Western Front in hot weather. The cigar in an elegant holder is a non-regulation item of equipment!

86▲

87▼

88. Turkish prisoners with Indian guards in Mesopotamia. The Turks in 'Mespot' wore the same uniform as those in the Dardanelles and Palestine campaigns: greenish-khaki tunic and trousers, puttees, and the greyish-khaki cloth helmet styled an *enverieh* or 'Enver Pasha helmet', named from its designer, Enver Pasha himself, who it was said made a personal fortune out of its patent!

89. The Arab Revolt contributed considerably to Turkish discomfiture in the Middle East, and though many of the Arab troops eventually wore items of British uniform, civilian 'native' dress was most common, sometimes with a mixture of European-style garments (as at the right). The Sheikh of Mohommerah and his retainers illustrated wear the *kafiyah* head-dress, the long *dishdash* shirt and sometimes the long *abah* coat over the top, with an abundance of cartridge-belts and daggers. Firearms included British Lee-Enfields, captured Turkish Mausers and even Japanese Ariakas (supplied by Britain early in the Arab Revolt), but those illustrated carry the old British single-shot Martini-Henry.

90. The campaigns against the Germans in East Africa were conducted largely by British Empire forces. Illustrated here are two members of the 4th (Uganda) Battalion of the King's African Rifles, a splendid force formed in 1902 by the amalgamation of the Central Africa, Uganda and East Africa Rifles; 22 battalions served in the war. They wear the service uniform of light khaki jumper and shorts, khaki pillbox cap and brown leather equipment; many preferred bare feet for active service. The diminutive figure in the centre is a rifleman of the 2nd Jammu and Kashmir Infantry, one of the 'Imperial Service' units supplied by the loyal Indian states. Kashmir provided three infantry regiments, the 1st Infantry and 3rd Rifles serving in Palestine, and the 2nd and 3rd in East Africa.

▲88 ▼89

91. German signwriters at work, presumably a short distance from the front line. Trench nameboards and grave-markers gave such personnel a surfeit of work; the man on the right is finishing the decoration of a memorial cross to private Willy Pippig, apparently a member of the Hanoverian *Jäger-Battalion Nr. 10*

(Hannoversches), killed in October 1915.

92. A burial on the field of battle. Wherever possible the civilities were observed including burial in marked graves (albeit temporary ones: most were disinterred and laid to rest in proper cemeteries in due course), but all too often

proper burial was impossible, hence the huge numbers of men posted as 'missing, believed killed' who to this day have no known grave. The burial-party here are Australians, for once with no sign of the favourite slouch hat; steel helmets, some with fabric covers (as at the left) are carried instead.

90▲　　　　　　　　　　　　　91▲　92▼

The *Fotofax* series

A new range of pictorial studies of military subjects for the modeller, historian and enthusiast. Each title features a carefully-selected set of photographs plus a data section of facts and figures on the topic covered. With line drawings and detailed captioning, every volume represents a succinct and valuable study of the subject. New and forthcoming titles:

Warbirds
F-111 Aardvark
P-47 Thunderbolt
B-52 Stratofortress
Stuka!
Jaguar
US Strategic Air Power:
  Europe 1942–1945
Dornier Bombers
RAF in Germany

Vintage Aircraft
German Naval Air Service
Sopwith Camel
Fleet Air Arm, 1920–1939
German Bombers of WWI

Soldiers
World War One: 1914
World War One: 1915
World War One: 1916
Union Forces of the American
  Civil War
Confederate Forces of the
  American Civil War
Luftwaffe Uniforms
British Battledress 1945–1967
  (2 vols)

Warships
Japanese Battleships, 1897–
  1945
Escort Carriers of World War
  Two
German Battleships, 1897–
  1945
Soviet Navy at War, 1941–1945
US Navy in World War Two,
  1943–1944
US Navy, 1946–1980 (2 vols)
British Submarines of World
  War One

Military Vehicles
The Chieftain Tank
Soviet Mechanized Firepower
  Today
British Armoured Cars since
  1945
NATO Armoured Fighting
  Vehicles
The Road to Berlin
NATO Support Vehicles

The *Illustrated* series

The internationally successful range of photo albums devoted to current, recent and historic topics, compiled by leading authors and representing the best means of obtaining your own photo archive.

Warbirds
US Spyplanes
USAF Today
Strategic Bombers, 1945–1985
Air War over Germany
Mirage
US Naval and Marine Aircraft
  Today
USAAF in World War Two
B-17 Flying Fortress
Tornado
Junkers Bombers of World War
  Two
Argentine Air Forces in the
  Falklands Conflict
F-4 Phantom Vol II
Army Gunships in Vietnam
Soviet Air Power Today
F-105 Thunderchief
Fifty Classic Warbirds
Canberra and B-57
German Jets of World War Two

Vintage Warbirds
The Royal Flying Corps in
  World War One
German Army Air Service in
  World War One
RAF between the Wars
The Bristol Fighter
Fokker Fighters of World War
  One
Air War over Britain, 1914–
  1918
Nieuport Aircraft of World War
  One

Tanks
Israeli Tanks and Combat
  Vehicles
Operation Barbarossa
Afrika Korps
Self-Propelled Howitzers
British Army Combat Vehicles
  1945 to the Present
The Churchill Tank
US Mechanized Firepower
  Today
Hitler's Panzers
Panzer Armee Afrika
US Marine Tanks in World War
  Two

Warships
The Royal Navy in 1980s
The US Navy Today
NATO Navies of the 1980s
British Destroyers in World
  War Two
Nuclear Powered Submarines
Soviet Navy Today
British Destroyers in World
  War One
The World's Aircraft Carriers,
  1914–1945
The Russian Convoys, 1941–
  1945
The US Navy in World War
  Two
British Submarines in World
  War Two
British Cruisers in World War
  One
U-Boats of World War Two
Malta Convoys, 1940–1943

Uniforms
US Special Forces of World
  War Two
US Special Forces 1945 to the
  Present
The British Army in Northern
  Ireland
Israeli Defence Forces, 1948 to
  the Present
British Special Forces, 1945 to
  Present
US Army Uniforms Europe,
  1944–1945
The French Foreign Legion
Modern American Soldier
Israeli Elite Units
US Airborne Forces of World
  War Two
The Boer War
The Commandos World War
  Two to the Present
Victorian Colonial Wars

A catalogue listing these series and other Arms & Armour Press titles is available on request from: Sales Department, Arms & Armour Press, Artillery House, Artillery Row, London SW1P 1RT.